Mud Racing

Jeff Savage

Capstone Press
MINNEAPOLIS

Printed in the United States of America.

Capstone Press • 2440 Fernbrook Lane • Minneapolis, MN 55447

Editorial Director   John Coughlan
Managing Editor   John Martin
Production Editor   James Stapleton
Copy Editor   Thomas Streissguth

Library of Congress Cataloging-in-Publication Data

Savage, Jeff, 1961--
  Mud Racing / Jeff Savage
    p. cm.
  Includes bibliographical references (p.) and index.
  Summary: Presents a brief history of mud racing; describes the preparation needed, the types of vehicles involved, the mud pit, and happenings at a main event; concludes with a glossary of terms.
    ISBN 1-56065-257-8
    1. Mud racing--Juvenile literature. [1. Mud racing. 2. Racing.] I. Title.
  GV1029.9.M83S28   1996
  796.7'2--dc20   95-7127
                                                    CIP
                                                    AC

99 98 97 96 95   6 5 4 3 2 1

Table of Contents

Chapter 1
A Great Mud Race

Alvin Esh was nervous. He sat in his truck, *Beef T Blue*, in the **pit area** of the indoor arena. People surrounded him. Thousands of excited mud-racing fans packed the stands. This was the last racing event of the year.

The Main Event

Fifteen mud racers would race once through the mud pit. The fastest four would advance to the **shootout**. The other 11 would be eliminated.

Mud-racing vehicles are built to zip through slippery sand and mucky mud.

The main event began. Tony Farrell's vehicle, *Blue Ribbon Bandit*, spun its tires at the starting line. Byron Tinkey's blue coupe, *Bad Habit*, hit a rut and rolled over. Jeff Sterkin's yellow-and-red racer, *Devastation*, slid off the track. Jeremy Finley's red vehicle, *S Kicker*, went airborne and flipped over.

The drivers were all wearing their seat belts, so nobody was hurt. But none of them qualified for the shootout.

Alvin Esch, in *Beef T Blue*, had better luck. Alvin powered through the mud to the finish line in less than two seconds.

Tom Martin in *Super Trooper*, Paul Shafer in *Mud Patrol*, and Matt Ward in *Mystic Warrior* were the other finalists.

The Shootout

Mystic Warrior was the first to race. Matt Ward sat behind the steering wheel. His father, Preston, helped line up the vehicle at the starting line.

The green light flashed, and Matt roared off the line. *Mystic Warrior* splashed into the mud pit and made it to the finish line in 1.72 seconds–a great time!

Super Trooper was next. Tom Martin, known to many as the Father of Mud Racing, had won the championship four years in a row.

This modified pickup sends sand flying as it moves down the track.

If anyone could beat Mat Ward's time, it was Tom Martin.

Tom waited at the starting line and revved his engine. But when the green signal flashed, *Super Trooper*'s tires spun out in the mud. *Super Trooper* churned through the pit but reached the finish line in a poor time–2.85 seconds.

It's Alvin's Turn

Alvin was next. He pulled his seat belt snug and gave a thumbs-up to the official starter. He stared at the pole of lights and took a deep breath. The green light flashed. *Beef T Blue* jumped off the line, and roared through the mud pit.

Alvin hung on. *Beef T Blue* blazed to the finish line, and Alvin hit the brakes. The crowd roared.

Alvin looked up at the scoreboard timer. The time blinked on–1.61 seconds! *Beef T Blue* was in first place.

Here Comes Mud Patrol

There was still one racer to go. It was Paul Shafer in *Mud Patrol*–the defending champion.

Drivers have to skillfully maneuver through deep tracks left by the other racers.

Paul studied the mud pit carefully and lined up *Mud Patrol*. Alvin Esch waited with his crew in the pit area. Alvin had turned in a good time with *Beef T Blue*. Would *Mud Patrol* be faster?

Mud Patrol got a great jump off the line. It roared into the mud pit at high speed. But then it hit a **tire rut**. *Mud Patrol* lurched to the left. Paul jerked the steering wheel to the right and brought *Mud Patrol* back on course. It reached the finish line safely, but its time was 1.94 seconds.

Alvin Esh had won the big race. *Beef T Blue* was the champion.

Safety comes first—so drivers always wear helmets.

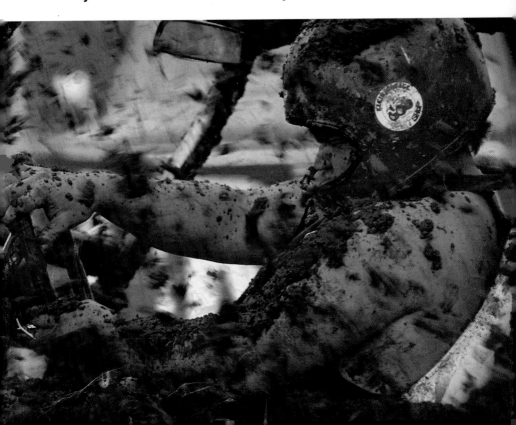

Chapter 2
The Basics

Mud racing is fast action. It takes a powerful engine and quick reflexes to win a mud race.

In mud racing, vehicles do not race at the same time or side by side. Instead, they take turns going through the mud pit. The vehicle that blasts through the pit fastest wins.

Mud racing is a newer sport compared to other motorsports. The first sanctioned races were held in the 1970s. Since that time, thousands of mud-racing events taken place in the United States and Canada.

Today, there are more than 200 indoor and outdoor mud-racing events in North America. Thousands of fans fill stadiums like the Metrodome in Minneapolis and the Skydome in Toronto to see the powerful engines, the great drivers, and the flying mud.

Before the Competition

To compete in a mud-racing event, drivers must first register their vehicles. They also must fill out waiver forms. Vehicles then are put through a **tech session,** in which an official inspects the vehicle's safety equipment. Then the vehicles are taken to the staging area.

At a drivers' meeting, safety rules are reviewed. Officials then use numbered balls, poker chips, or names pulled out of a hat to determine the racing order. Even an ordinary card deck has been used.

Competition Begins

In the first round, each vehicle races once through the mud pit. After all the vehicles have raced, their times are checked. The fastest vehicles earn the right to advance to the final round. Usually, the four fastest vehicles qualify for the final round. Sometimes, however, only the two fastest vehicles return for the final.

The final round is the big event. The vehicle that records the fastest time in the final round is the winner. First-round times do not count in determining the winner.

Getting a Second Chance

A driver sometimes gets a second chance. A **kill pin** on the back of each vehicle is connected by a tether cord to a pole at the starting line. When the vehicle reaches the finish line, an official pulls the cord tight and the kill pin is yanked out. This shuts off the engine. If the kill pin is pulled accidentally before his vehicle crosses the finish line, the driver gets to race again.

The driver sometimes decides that an area of the track is unsafe. He gets a second chance if he goes into an unsafe area.

A little mud won't stop this four-wheel machine.

Disqualification

There are three reasons for disqualification. A vehicle is disqualified if it does not stop within the stopping area beyond the finish line. A vehicle is also disqualified if the tether cord does not pull the kill pin, or if the kill pin is pulled but the engine does not shut off. Finally, a vehicle is disqualified if it goes out of bounds.

Track Officials

There are five race officials on the track. Three are at the starting area and two are near the finish line.

One official, the stager, holds the vehicle at the starting line. Another, the hookup man, connects the kill pin to the vehicle. A third, the starter, signals that the track is clear by waving a green flag or triggering a green light.

At the finish line, another hookup man reinserts the kill pin that is yanked out at the end of the race. The fifth official, a judge, determines if the vehicle has stayed in bounds and stopped within the stopping area.

Chapter 3
The History of Mud Racing

M ud racing is a combination of **sand dragging** and playing in the mud.

A popular motorsport, known as sand dragging, emerged in the 1960s. In sand dragging, dune buggies–vehicles built to race on sand–competed against each other in side-by-side competition. The motorsport was very popular on the beaches of California and Florida.

Meanwhile, in the Midwest, it became popular for drivers to race their pickup trucks in muddy fields. By the late 1970s, these drivers were using cars with souped-up engines. Mud racing grew out of these two motorsports.

Several organizations began to sponsor mud-racing events. Among them were USA Motorsports, the American Mud Racing Association, and SRO Motorsports.

Powering Through the Pit

At first, mud-racing vehicles were not strong enough to make it through the mud pit. The winner was the racer who traveled the farthest distance into the mud pit. After each try, the vehicle would have to be towed out of the mud.

Mud racers noticed the powerful engines used in other motorsports. In 1983, high-performance motors were introduced to mud racing. Vehicles now went all the way through the pit.

The rules then had to be changed. A finish line was needed at the end of the mud pit. Officials began timing vehicles with stop watches. Engines got bigger and bigger. Soon vehicles were blasting through the pit in just a few seconds.

Big Al Esh keeps a good grip on the slippery track.

A New Timing System

Hand timing was too slow for the powerful new mud racers. A timing system using an electronic beam, called the **Chrondek Timing System**, was introduced. A light-operated photo cell triggers a timing box at both the starting line and the finish line. This timing system records a vehicle's speed within one-thousandth of a second.

Chapter 4
Mud-Racing Vehicles

Many types of vehicles compete in mud-racing events. *Mud Patrol* is a car. *Beef T Blue* is a truck. *Mystic Warrior* is a white roadster. *Blew Max* is a blue jeep.

There are several classes of vehicles. The most important are open-class vehicles, cut-class vehicles, pro stock-class vehicles, and stock-class vehicles.

Open-Class Vehicles

Open-class vehicles can be almost any car or truck, and they can use any number of engines of any size. Popular high-performance engines include Janke, Hemi, and Arias. Aluminum **blowers** made by BDS or Littlefield are often added to pull in more air and increase performance.

Most open-class machines use standard racing alcohol fuel. Some vehicles still have **nitrous oxide**-injected motors. Nitrous oxide, however, is a very flammable fuel and is becoming unpopular with drivers. A cable-operated throttle system is used on nearly all open-class vehicles.

On open-class vehicles, tires cannot be more than 44 inches (1.1 meter) tall. There is no width limit. Tires called **scooper tires** are sometimes permitted on open-class vehicles. Scooper tires are drag-racing slicks with about a dozen six-inch (15-centimeter) cups vulcanized onto them. Because vehicles with scooper tires go so fast that they take longer to stop, scoopers have been illegal at indoor events since 1989.

Spectators keep their distance when the dirt is flying.

Cut-Class Vehicles

The difference between open-class vehicles and cut-class vehicles is the tires. Cut-class vehicles use only tires approved by the Department of Transportation. These are called **DOT tires**. Among popular tires are Bigger Diggers, Mickey Thompsons, Dick Cepeks,

27

Somehow, John Lynam keeps his *Mudslinger* pickup nice and clean as he moves it through the course.

Firestones, and BF Goodriches. Drivers use grinders and saws to cut tire tread for better traction.

Pro Stock-Class Vehicles

Pro stocks are generally full-bodied vehicles such as jeeps, pickups, Chevy Blazers, and

Ford Broncos. These vehicles can use high-performance engines but not blowers.

The tires on pro stock-class vehicles cannot be modified. Only DOT tires are permitted.

Stock-Class Vehicles

Stocks are vehicles that have not been modified. They compete just as they came from the manufacturer. Stock vehicles are street legal and can be driven around town.

An Expensive Motorsport

Mud-racing vehicles can be expensive. A driver might spend as much as $120,000 to build and maintain an open-class vehicle. Stock vehicles, on the other hand, cost only what the dealer charges.

Chapter 5

The Mud Pit and the Stopping Area

It takes a good mud pit to have a successful mud race.

Building a Mud Pit

There's more to building a mud pit than mixing water with dirt. A good mud pit has the right amounts of dirt, water, sand, and sawdust. In 1990, track builder John Reynolds found just the right combination. And it's still used today. The recipe calls for one-third water, one-third sawdust, one-sixth dirt, and one-sixth sand.

Drivers have to keep steady control to avoid a dangerous spinout.

It takes a lot of earth-moving equipment to build a mud pit. Bulldozers, front-end loaders, Bobcats (four-wheeled uniloaders), and backhoes are required.

The Size of the Mud Pit

The mud pit is also known as the mud bog. An indoor mud pit is usually 80 feet (24.4

meters) long, 12 feet (3.6 meters) wide, and about three feet (90 centimeters) deep. An outdoor mud bog is usually from 100 to 250 feet (30.5 to 76.5 meters) long and 15 to 30 feet (4.5 to 9 meters) wide.

The starting line is usually about three feet (90 centimeters) from the front of the pit. The finish line is about one foot (30 centimeters) from the end of the pit.

The Stopping Area

All mud-racing tracks have a stopping area. It is an important part of a track. Racing vehicles that do not stop within the stopping area are disqualified. For indoor tracks, the stopping area is equal in length to the mud pit. For outdoor tracks, the stopping area is one and a half times as long as the pit.

For an indoor track, then, the mud pit and the stopping area each might be 80 feet (24.4 meters). For an outdoor track, if the mud pit is 200 feet (61 meters) long, the stopping area must be 300 feet (91.5 meters).

Chapter 6

The Drivers and the Circuit

All mud-racing drivers share common interests. They love cars, engines, and mud. Anyone with a driver's license can compete in mud racing. Matt Ward became a mud racer at 16. Some of Matt's competitors are over 50 years old.

Mud racers might be mechanics, electricians, shop owners, or construction workers. While most mud racers are men, some women do compete.

Two cool racers fly down the track in a dead heat.

Strategy

The secret in mud racing is to know the mud pit. The first racer can plow through the mud bog without worry. But ruts begin to form as the event continues. The best drivers study the way each vehicle goes through the pit. Then the driver chooses the path to drive.

Before going into the mud pit, the driver revs the engine of his vehicle. He pushes down on the **accelerator** pedal with his right foot while stepping hard on the brake pedal with his left foot. The engine revs loudly. The green light blinks on and signals the driver to go. He lifts his left foot off the brake and steps hard on the accelerator with his right foot. The vehicle shoots forward.

The driver aims his vehicle and holds on. The vehicle slams into the mud pit. It shakes violently. The driver's head is pressed back against the **roll bar**. His vision is blurred. The race is over in seconds. The driver hasn't even had time to blink.

Big Mud-Racing Events

Among the biggest mud-racing events are the World Finals at the Houston Astrodome and events at the Delta Center in Salt Lake City, the RCA Dome in Indianapolis, and the Mid-South

Drivers put a lot of work and money into their vehicles.

Coliseum in Memphis. A winner's check at one of these major events is worth as much as $10,000. Points, too, are awarded at each event.

Circuits

Circuits are made up of a number of events in different locations over the course of a season or year. SRO Motorsports, USA

Motorsports, and the American Mud Racing Association are some of the organizers of mud-racing circuits in North America.

Each mud-racing circuit has its own point system. Drivers earn points at every event on the circuit. Circuits also offer winning drivers special prize money on top of the purses they can win at individual events.

But it's worth it, because winning a mud race can bring in as much as $10,000.

Chapter 7

Safety

Mud-racing drivers know there is something more important than winning. That is safety.

Drivers wear helmets made of a hard plastic material called **Kevlar**. They wear fireproof suits made of **flame-retardant** cotton material. They wear safety belts across their laps and **shoulder harnesses** across their chests. All vehicles have a fire extinguisher in the cab.

The Roll Bar

All mud-racing vehicles have **roll bars**. A roll bar is a thick metal pipe that goes above and around the driver. If the vehicle rolls over, the roll bar keeps the roof from collapsing.

Vehicles are also equipped with a **transmission blanket**. This keeps exploding engine parts from flying into the crowd. A **scattershield** surrounds the block. A **blowershield** is around the blower. These also protect against flying parts. A **throttle-return spring** keeps the accelerator pedal from sticking.

Safety Crews

A medical crew and a fire crew are present at every mud race. Two licensed emergency medical technicians stand by with an ambulance. The fire crew consists of four people who operate the fire equipment needed in the case of a crash.

These safety crews rush to the scene when crashes occur. They were at Skydome in Toronto when Tony Farrell's vehicle, *Blue Ribbon Bandit*, popped a wheelie, turned sideways, went through the mud pit on one wheel, flipped over at the finish line, and caught fire.

The medical crew made sure Tony was not hurt. The fire crew quickly doused the fire with extinguishers and fire hoses.

Glossary

accelerator–the foot pedal controlling the flow of fuel to the engine

blower–an aluminum device that pulls air into the engine. It is also called a supercharger.

blowershield–a device surrounding the blower that prevents exploding engine parts from flying into the crowd

Chrondek Timing System–a timing system in which a light-operated photo cell triggers a timing box at both the starting line and finish line. This system records speeds to within one-thousandth of a second.

circuit–a series of events in which points are awarded

DOT tires–tires approved by the Department of Transportation

flame-retardant–slow to catch fire

Kevlar–a hard plastic material used to make protective helmets

kill pin–a metal pin on the back of each vehicle connected by a tether cord to a pole at the starting line. When the vehicle reaches the finish line, the kill pin is yanked, shutting off the engine.

nitrous oxide–a gas added to fuel to provide a boost to the engine

pit area–the area where drivers prepare their vehicles for the mud race

roll bar–a protective bar (usually made of steel pipe) above and around the driver that prevents the roof of a vehicle from collapsing in a rollover

sand dragging–a motorsport in which dune buggies race on sand

scattershield–a shield surrounding the engine block; used to prevent exploding parts from flying into the crowd

scooper tires–drag-racing tires that have a dozen or so six-inch (15-centimeter) cups vulcanized onto them to provide better traction

shootout–a final competition in which the fastest mud racers shoot for first place

shoulder harness–a protective belt that extends across a driver's chest from shoulder to lap

tech session–an inspection of the mud-racing vehicles by an official. Each vehicle must have certain mechanical and safety features to pass teching."

tire rut–a groove in the mud pit or elsewhere on the track created by a vehicle's tire

throttle return spring–a device that controls the amount of fuel sent from the tank to the cylinder. Some mud racers have a throttle system on the steering wheel, instead of a pedal on the floor.

transmission blanket–a shield that wraps around the transmission to keep exploding engine parts from flying into the crowd

To Learn More

Atkinson, E.J. *Monster Vehicles.* Mankato, MN: Capstone Press, 1991.

Holder, Bill and Harry Dunn. *Monster Wheels.* New York: Sterling Publishing, 1990.

Johnson, Scott. *Monster Truck Racing.* Minneapolis: Capstone Press, 1994.

Johnson, Scott. *The Original Monster Truck: Bigfoot.* Minneapolis: Capstone Press, 1994.

Savage, Jeff. *Demolition Derby.* Minneapolis: Capstone Press, 1995.

———. *Monster Truck Wars.* Minneapolis: Capstone Press, 1995.

———. *Truck and Tractor Pulling.* Minneapolis: Capstone Press, 1995.

Sullivan, George. *Here Come the Monster Trucks.* New York: Cobblehill Books, 1989.

Some Useful Addresses

Monster Truck Racing Association
6311 N Lindbergh
Hazelwood, MO 63042

National Mud Racing Association (NMRA)
Rt. 1, Box 8380
Palatka, FL 32177

National Mud Racing Organization (NMRO)
5542 State Rt. 68 South
Urbana, OH 43078

SRO Motorsports
477 E Butterfield Road
Suite 400
Lombard, IL 60148

USA Motorsports
2310 W 75th Street
Prarie Village, KS 66208

Index